My Life as a Time Traveller

a Memoir in 18 Discrete Fragments

Oz Hardwick

First published 2023 by The Hedgehog Poetry Press

Published in the UK by
The Hedgehog Poetry Press
Coppack House, 5
Churchill Avenue
Clevedon
BS21 6QW

www.hedgehogpress.co.uk

ISBN: 978-1-916830-04-2

Copyright © Oz Hardwick 2023

The right of Oz Hardwick to be identified as the author of this work has been asserted in accordance with the Copyright, Designs and Patents Act 1988.

All rights reserved. No part of this publication may be reproduced, stored in or introduced into a retrieval system, or transmitted in any form, or by any means (electronic, mechanical, photocopying, recording or otherwise) without prior written permissions of the publisher. Any person who does any unauthorised act in relation to this publication may be liable for criminal prosecution and civil claims for damages,

9 8 7 6 5 4 3 2 1

A CIP Catalogue record for this book is available from the British Library.

Cover image © Oz Hardwick

Author photograph © Susan Whitehouse

Dedicated to all the selves we've left behind and all those who, in spite of time and circumstance, stay.

Contents

Regression Point 7
Daphne in the Edgelands 8
Mail-Order Mysteries 9
Jet-lag in the Rust Belt 10
New Wave 11
Adventures in the Art World 12
Safe Harbour 13
Conceptual Parenting for the Unprepared 14
How Many Miles to Babylon? 15
Shell 16
Cloudburst 17
Hooray for Hollywood 18
The Darkest Hour and a Half 19
Nights at the Flood Plain Buffet 20
Painting by Numbers 21
Self-Assessment 22
Patriotism and the Great Schism 23
Dodo Makes Plans 24

Regression Point

When I was bud, I was tremble. I was tight yes and the ah of near petal. Leafshade and therefore. Complexity. I was a situation, a scenario: the possibility of, the likelihood of. Stretch and press. I was more than, other than, and the same as. Fold and touch. Simple intricacy. I was the still oh of inevitable and the what of if. Convolution. I was bud the potential. The conundrum. Bud was the me of me.

Daphne in the Edgelands

When I was leaves, I adopted the habits of leaves: their gait, their accents, their tastes in music and cinema. I buzzed late-night Metros with caffeine and carbohydrate molecules, green in flickering neon, a superhero in my own comic book: Captain Chloroplast, Saviour of the World. Now, high on a black whim, I am wood, fossilising into stone, becoming static balance, archivist of green. I know what I like and it is all my own: a Realist novel with neither character nor conclusion; a looped tape, echoing itself. A crow clatters by, holy wafer locked in its cynical beak; yet green becomes green, remains green, enacts the green that rides the night bus, building conurbations as it goes.

Mail-Order Mysteries

When I was small, I grew a desert from seeds I bought from an ad in the back of a comic. Other kids bought X-ray specs or kryptonite, but I'd been caught by the Hollywood magic, with the swoop and sigh of dunes, and swathes of rich silk billowing around dark eyes beneath skies the colour of dazzling invitations. I grew it in a pot in grandad's greenhouse, between the tomatoes and his prize gloxinias, as close to the Sun as the northern winter allowed. I'd sit there after school with my homework - Victorian poetry or the decline of the British Empire - and watch oases form, while nomadic tribes lit out across trackless gold, singing songs by Sigmund Romberg. It all changed on my 14th birthday when they discovered oil, bringing cars, casinos, and hotels, linen suits, and chilled mint drinks sipped as the Sun slipped below the horizon. The house, I'm told, is gone, and I probably wouldn't even recognise the town, but the desert's still there. I've seen it as a setting for Si-Fi movies and glossy ad campaigns, its persuasive mystery charming cash from dream-struck late night channel surfers. I look at my hand through X-ray specs. It glows like kryptonite.

Jet-lag in the Rust Belt

When I became old enough to forget my age, I returned to the lake with its swans and scholars. The sky was the colour of aluminium, the water rucked like molten solder, and trees were rivets to stop the land rolling away. But in all this industry, grey men in white robes, with beards dangling down to the fourteenth century, weighed the wounds and the sins, recalibrating the secular/religious divide, as women in home spun habits enumerated the sores and salves of the body politic. I listened to the voices raised in debate, and to the clash of nature welding itself to phenomenological assumptions: and between these familiar sounds, a swan sang a song from a time before I sought out awkward questions, from a time when I thought I knew what was going on.

New Wave

When I stepped into the square it was snowing like a film I saw in the 70s in an arts centre or an art school studio. There was a Polish woman with a fur collar and eyes like a young dog, with silver flakes glittering in her mussed-up hair and a cigarette forgotten in her dangling hand. Wolves sulked in shop doorways and the cobbles rang like a detuned piano in a bar full of boasting soldiers. Rose petals lay frozen beneath a sheen of significance and a child in fingerless gloves tore a black loaf to feed sparrows at the edge of a baroque fountain. The woman looked at her reflection and saw only wolves. The soldiers looked at the woman and saw only a child. The cigarette burned down and fell to the snowy ground as petals thawed and became sparrows. We talked about its significance in a café in the square, myself and the Polish woman. I think there were wolves and children. *Were you in the film?* I asked, but she offered me a cigarette instead of an answer. It was winter and the ash turned to snow as it fell.

Adventures in the Art World

When I sat down in the gallery, I merely wanted to take the weight off my aching knees, to rest my frazzled responses of dazzled awe between Old Master, Old Master, Old Master, *ad infinitum*. I didn't intend my stillness to be a statue, my unflinching realism praised, my provenance contested, and my likeness reproduced on tea towels and erasers. I simply sensed a dip in my blood sugar levels: the furtive Mars bar was *not* performance art, teasing the constraints of bovine complicity beneath the *No Eating* sign "like a cheeky, provincial Hermann Nitsch" (The Guardian). And when I dropped the wrapper, it was an accident: I didn't even notice, much less intend it to be an installation, "its casual lack of artifice an ironic affront to fragile Wokeness to be read in the long, messy shadow of Tracey Emin's Bed" (The Sunday Times). I had no thoughts of MBE or FRA, no expectation of a BBC documentary, Turner Prize, or retrospectives in major European cities. No, nothing premeditated at all. I'd always thought of myself as more of a prose poet.

Safe Harbour

When I opened the book, I found something I'd forgotten writing, its words struggling on the page, negotiating the unpredictable tides between the permanent and the transient, like a moth with the Ten Commandments – or Hamlet's soliloquy, or maybe the names of the 1966 England squad – tattooed across its wings. These flimsy covers are an apt harbour, but I know I must tear out the page, fold it into an origami funeral boat, and launch it blazing from a beach I've only seen in holiday brochures.

Conceptual Parenting for the Unprepared

When I slid the children out of the freezer, they hadn't changed at all; except maybe their names. The one who used to be called David or Joshua was now called something less biblical, like Edward. Another one was called Sophie, and may always have been, though I don't think so. The other two just had numbers, but I was never good with figures, and I can't remember where I wrote them down. That's the thing with children: one day they're helping in the garden, or learning to colour inside the lines, then the next they're lying amongst the desserts and frozen veg. I like to read to them: mainly instruction manuals, but also paint catalogues and chess problems. I've tried every kind of fiction, from Henry James to E. L. James, but you never know where you are with all the plots and characters skating between icy faces. Once I tried *The Nation's Favourite Poems* but got as far as Yeats and just tossed the book down the stairs.

How Many Miles to Babylon?

When I cut the wire, the lights go out, all phones are dead, and puppet policemen slump at their posts. There's a hole in the fence that's just big enough to crawl through if I leave absolutely everything behind; so I fold my clothes with my house and family and leave them on the last park bench for whoever they may fit, and I bury my cash and my wedding ring beside crude wax poppets to mess with future archaeologists. The sky is creased with cold and searchlights, and armed guards bristle in each angular shadow, but I know to keep my nose low and my raw elbows shuffling in time with the ticking of the clock at the heart of my repressed memories. Come the clear morning, a phone will ring in the back room of a cut-price jeweller's and armed guards will replace the city's every lightbulb, but I'll be long gone, holed up in a hall of mirrors and dressed like an archaeologist from between the wars, with a private income and leather patches on my tweed elbows. I'll wire my wife to tell her of wonderful things, but she'll tell me she's single and threaten to call the police.

Shell

When I open my inbox there's a handful of shells. Some days there's the sea and a fleet of white sails either coming or going, a child reaching to pull a red ball from the sky, and a glitter of stones licked by waves. Other days there's the wasteland and a fleet of burnt-out cars going nowhere, an old man reaching to touch the hem of a passing nurse, and a glitter of blind eyes beneath oil. I read updates like a clairvoyant reads minds, closing my eyes and making something up that sounds plausible – perceptive, even – regardless of circumstances. Some days it's a Whit Monday charabanc ride with my grandmother wreathed in cotton flowers. Other days its postcards from her brothers and war graves standing row-on-row to the twisted margin of the world. Either way, it's a call for gritty coffee and expensive biscuits, an excuse to spark up a rollie as I press Delete. The cat curls into the precise shape of my inbox, while I tiptoe on eggshells until they crack open into baby snakes, green as mould and thin as pencils.

Cloudburst

When I see the rain watching me, I can't meet its gaze. I look at my feet as they sink into the ground and look at the lake that wasn't there last night. Soldiers in shabby drab row makeshift rafts, as if they are asleep, or as if they are clockwork automata in an abandoned fairground. Though I still can't raise my eyes, I can feel the rain staring at me – *like stair rods*, as my grandmother would say – and I remember flying downstairs four steps at a time, my feet a silver blur, as the siren stripped the roof and the weatherman choked on the news he couldn't impart. I am waist deep in waterlogged ground, waiting for the rain to pass and for the soldiers to arrive with illegal armaments and foreign aid, and I remember flying downstairs four steps at a time, my brain a red blur, as the postman knocked on my birthday morning. The soldiers drag their rafts ashore, the ground swallows me whole, and I remember rain pouring downstairs before resolutely looking the other way.

Hooray for Hollywood

When I take my shoes off, my feet stay inside them, and I resign myself to it being one of those nights, so I take to the sofa with a microwave meal, a bottle of water, hand sanitiser, a year's supply of toilet rolls, and the cat. The cat distrusts the smell of hand sanitiser but is drawn by the warm chicken, and the mound of quilted tissue makes a comfortable nest with enough height to afford a sense of security. There's no signal to the television, so I replay favourite films in my head, looking out for bit-part actors who would later have their own stars on the Hollywood Walk of Fame. The cat mews and shuffles in its sleep as the door opens and closes, my feet letting themselves out and striding into the world. I fall into broken sleep, in which I dream I am a bit-part actor in Rick's, miming *La Marseillaise* after claiming I could sing at the audition. When my head finally clears, I attribute it to imposter syndrome and Anti-Nazi League gigs in the 80s. The cat's off doing cat stuff, and I retune the television, bringing into focus an entertainment show, where my feet are pressing themselves into damp cement to the accompaniment of rattling shutters and old-fashioned flashbulbs. I cleanse my hands of the whole affair, but through the melee I'm sure I can see the cat trying on my shoes.

The Darkest Hour and a Half

When I wrap myself in this worn sheet, I recall my mother's soothing tone, her reassurances that there was nothing but night beneath the bed, nothing but the world behind the door. I scrunch myself smaller than a child, smaller than a fist or an eye squeezed shut, burrow deep into iron springs and cream ticking, hide from the crow in the blind chimney, the insect drum on tired lino. If I had a mouth I'd scream, and if my limbs weren't knotted I'd run, but these are things I never thought I'd need again, so I offer myself to the syncopation of clocks and the anticipation of dripping taps. The night will soon end, with the world not too far behind it, and I cling to the sheet like grit in a waking eye while, between the first car on the street and the dawn chorus of alarms, the room disperses around me, forgetting the shape of sleep.

Nights at the Flood Plain Buffet

When I'm wanting sleep, I'm a hungry river, piling my plate high, elbowing my way to the lushest cuts. There's grease on my chin, there are flies in my eyes, and my small talk's a fishhook snagged in a shopping trolley. I'm the suck and grab beneath bridges, the frigid shock on the hottest day on record. I am safety notices stripped of meaning and the outlines of rigid bodies still pressed into casual ripples. When I'm wanting sleep, my lock gates snap like stale fortune cookies, and everything that isn't water sweeps through: diamond rings, dynamite, the disenfranchisement of the working class, and dead eels by the salted barrel-load. Small boats fold like ironic applause. A golden leaf spirals and dances. Reflections bow like obsequious waiters, waiting as I'm wanting, as wading birds clip chopstick beaks that snap from spring to sea. I lick my fingers clean as sleep slips beneath the surface like a shivering child. Both our bellies are empty, aching.

Painting by Numbers

When I close my eyes, everything is that colour between Sunday night and Monday morning, when the sacred has been left behind and the ink and oil of the city are already staining my fingertips. It's the colour of all those thoughts that come and go as I'm brushing my teeth or falling into my usual seat on the early train. It's the colour of all the voices that tell me I'm wrong, that I need to change. When I open my eyes, the day ahead is paint-by-numbers, with a neat *9* in every identical square. I dip the brush into the corner of my eye and paint each square in order, careful not to cross the lines. I consider number 9 in the context of John Lennon's oeuvre, emergency services, and German pronunciation; and I wonder what my grandmother – who could ward off door-to-door evangelists with her perfect recall of biblical minutiae – knows of divine completeness now that she rests in the presence of her Lord. By the time I finish, it is dark, I don't know what day it is, and I can't decide whether my eyes are open or closed.

Self-Assessment

When I reassess my position – that *long, hard look* advocated by self-appointed arbiters of all things pure and mutual – I discover myself in the wrong skin and all its concomitant displacements. Exhibit A: I am in a room full of glove puppets with stitched-on wide-eyed innocence and arms open to most possibilities, my mouth full of words that prevent me from telling the truth. There are certain expectations from all concerned, but I suspect that mine are somewhat different to the clowns, bears, and crocodiles ranked in rows before me. Exhibit B: When I check my phone it is anything but a phone. Sometimes it is a block of ice with an unused theatre ticket frozen inside, sometimes it is a book of discontinued savings stamps. On very rare occasions it is a lingering scent which I have been trying to describe since I first picked up a pencil. Exhibit C: The name on my office door has very little to do with me other than certain formal similarities of curve and line. The same may be said of photographs, fingerprints, and speech inflections. The same may be said of the years I've scraped into this too-tight skin – which I maybe put on in a flustered rush after that first occasion on which I fell apart in a red, red room full of clowns, bears, and crocodiles, though I can't for the life or death of me remember – to present the illusion of time. A glove puppet raises a wise brow but the hand inside is a child's, waiting to be led somewhere safe.

Patriotism and the Great Schism

When I look back years from now, I'll think of this as a time of hotel biros and school exercise books; of learning to write again once the printer ink ran out, and of learning semaphore to speak to strangers through windows they'd nailed shut. I'll remember how a house across the back lane raised flags, and how it took weeks for the wind to blow out the creases gathered in transit. I'll remember how I was sure I heard troops drilling to barked orders after dark, and how the ground shook to the deployment of heavy artillery, yet in the morning there was nothing but garden gnomes, a stone bridge over a pond, and the figure of a woodcutter who *chop chop chopped* at a plastic log. I'll think of this as a time of black organic apricots, tinned spaghetti shapes, and the assiduous tasseography that followed every makeshift meal, initiating disputes and alliances that we'll take to the grave. I'll study untidy writing that ignores the margins on narrow feint, and try to understand how any of it happened. Mostly, though, I'll think of this as a time of words rather than actions; of empty hotels resigning themselves to the sea, and of flags for countries I didn't even believe in.

Dodo Makes Plans

When I retire, I'll move back to the land of feathers, where birds flock together in hands and bushes. I'll cash in my nest egg and bear gold and white in many baskets. I'll walk upon shells. I'll catch every worm, early and late, and I'll make friends with the albatross around my neck. Crazy as a loon, I'll take to it all like a duke to water, proud as a peacock and elegant as a swan, with just my coronet glittering above the ripples.

www.ingramcontent.com/pod-product-compliance
Lightning Source LLC
Chambersburg PA
CBHW020141130526
44590CB00041B/633